Talk Football

Sharing Jesus through talking the beautiful game

By Ambassadors Football

Edited by Rob Taylor

AMBASSADORS
FOOTBALL

Foreword

It was the 28th April 1990. I was six years old. I walked up the claret and blue painted steps. Even before I saw the pitch, tingles ran down my spine and every hair on my body was on end at the sound of the roaring crowd. The sight of the green grass and seeing the players walk out for the first time gave me a surge of adrenaline and joy I had never experienced before. I am not sure how I coped when that first goal went in.

Me and my mates broke our family sofa celebrating a Champions League winner. Though I say so myself, I have scored some goals that I hope to see action replays of when I get to heaven. My knees have not quite been the same after I was part of the team that once broke the world record for the world's longest 5-a-side football match. To my wife's dismay I can recall the memories of some matches as well as our wedding day or the birth of my children.

I believe football is God-given.

The beautiful game was instituted by beautiful people – their sense of creativity, competition and collaboration instilled in them by a beautiful God who made them in his image. Our imagination and inventiveness are a reflection of our divine imprint. Football has the power to bring out the best in people – the sportsmanship of England manager Gareth Southgate comforting the Colombian Mateus Uribe after his penalty miss at the 2018 World Cup and the unity around the Black Lives Matter movement. It has the astonishing capacity to unify a town and community in elation or grief. It has the capability to bond permanently two people who have nothing in common apart from the club they support.

I'm a bit passionate about it.

But there is at least one thing that I am more passionate about. His name is Jesus.

There's a famous misquote attributed to late Liverpool manager Bill Shankly: 'Some people think football is a matter of life and death. I assure you, it's much more serious than that.' The good news is that football really isn't *that* important. The better news is that following Jesus or not is a matter of life and death. And he brings life.

Knowing Jesus is the best thing in the world. The message that he we are loved beyond our wildest expectations, can be forgiven for our failures, know the presence of God in our present and have hope for the future is good news - worthy of all our devotion and passion. Being reconciled to God changes everything. I have experienced this in my own life. Insecurity has been replaced with the firm foundation that I have nothing to lose and nothing to prove. A need to impress has been replaced with an assurance that there is nothing I can do to make God love me more, or less. As tragedy has struck and I have experienced bereavement and disappointment, I have known the presence of God with me in the darkest of valleys. You never walk alone.

The danger of football is that it can become an idol in our lives. We can worship the created rather than the Creator. I have certainly allowed my passion for sport to exceed that of my Saviour. In late 2014, I felt so convicted and challenged by how important it had become that I decided to fast from watching, playing, thinking and talking about all sport for a year. 2015 was a barren desert of sport-less activity. My wife describes it as one of the best years of her life. New Year's Day 2016 was one of the best days ever.

But in its rightful place, football is not only a source of great joy and pleasure for us, it is also an indisputably brilliant tool for mission. I have witnessed its power to create bonds between individuals, through which the gospel has been shared. I have seen its ability to gather a crowd to hear the good news who would not be seen anywhere near a church building. (I once preached the gospel at an outreach event after tearing my cruciate ligament in the preceding match. I really did suffer for Jesus that day!) I have watched gifted evangelists masterfully use footballing analogies to communicate the heart of God in language that connects with an audience who think the most famous Jesus is a Manchester City forward and that Moses plays at wing back.

Ambassadors Football are a beautiful organisation seeking to see the most beautiful message in the world reach people through the beautiful game. *Talk Football* takes gospel themes and expertly weaves them into modern, relevant and engaging footballing narratives and images. I've known Rob Taylor for nearly 20 years. He is the real deal. He is an excellent footballer with a sweet left foot and we have shared the triumphs and tragedy of being fellow Aston Villa fans throughout our friendship. I'm a big fan of his. But most importantly, he loves Jesus and is sold out for him.

It was Karl Barth who said that the preacher should hold the newspaper in one hand and the Bible in the other.

Jesus used his surroundings to illustrate the profound divine truths of the universe. I have no doubt that *Talk Football* will be used in a variety of settings to clearly communicate gospel themes to generations of fans who idolise the sport we love, but are crying out for hope.

We are good news people in a bad news world. We must continue to use whatever tools we have at our disposal to tell the greatest story ever. My prayer is that many get hold of this great resource and use it winsomely, relevantly and passionately to share Jesus in sweaty sports halls and singing stadia, on astroturf and muddy pitches, under floodlights and the baking sun, home and away. I thank God for football and I pray that sports evangelists and pastors play their part in the revival that we long for in the UK.

Even from this short foreword you can probably tell I get pretty loud in the stands in support of my team. I love roaring, 'COME ON!' at the top of my lungs. As you take these talks and use them for God's glory, I'm standing with you, cheering you on. Let's together see many lives transformed in Jesus' name.

How, then, can they call on the one they have not believed in? And how can they believe in the one of whom they have not heard? And how can they hear without someone preaching to them? And how can anyone preach unless they are sent? As it is written: "How beautiful are the feet of those who bring good news!" Romans 10:14-15

I'm urging you forward.

COME ON!!!

Phil Knox is Head of Mission to Young Adults for the Evangelical Alliance

About *Talk Football*

Football is a great gatherer of people. Be it watching, playing or coaching, millions of people in Britain have a weekly routine built around football.

For Christians, football gives us opportunities to worship God. From this place of worship we are compelled to go the extra mile, be salt and light and to love practically. One of the most encouraging movements of recent decades has been more and more churches recognising and supporting the calling that so many Christians have to honour God in their sport, and to show the love of Jesus to others as they do it.

For many, talking about their faith is difficult. We work hard to love and serve, but when chances arrive to say why we do it, we struggle to find the right words, or revert to churchy concepts and language that most people just don't understand.

For the past 10 years, Ambassadors Football have been trying to bridge that gap between football and faith through *Talk Football*. We send short weekly emails on an aspect of Christianity, expressed through a football lens. Common uses for *Talk Football* have included:

- Pre-match or half-time discussions at football trainings or matches
- Personal reflections for those exploring faith
- 'Water cooler' conversations with work colleagues
- School assemblies
- Talks at organised events like sports quizzes, seeker services or evangelistic tournaments

Talk Football is written by a whole range of people, from players to coaches to church leaders, all united by a love for football, and above all a love for Jesus.

We've carefully curated our library of articles to produce 25 short talks that are ready to use. They all take around 5 minutes to read, and can be used for a variety of audiences. We've listed them by title, theme, football references and Bible verses used here:

Talk	Themes	References	Verses
1.I'm Available, Gaffer	Invite	Man Utd, Gareth Bale	2 Corinthians 4.7; Acts 4.13
2.You Won't Get Sacked!	Value, patience	Chelsea, Frank Lampard	1 Peter 1.18-19; Psalm 103.8
3.Just a Mistake	Sin, forgiveness	Steven Gerrard	Romans 6.23
4.Who Would You Pick?	Grace	England, Gareth Southgate	Ephesians 2.8-9
5.Spiritually Skint or God's Grace?	Grace, Kingdom	European Super League	Matthew 5.4-5
6. Great Save	Salvation	Goalkeepers	Romans 10.9-13
7.Hope for the Future	Transformation	Newcastle, takeovers	Ephesians 2.3-5
8.Writing on the Wall	Sin and salvation	Manager sackings	Daniel 5; Romans 3.23
9.The God of Second Chances	Injustice, salvation	Christian Eriksen	Luke 4.18-19
10.World Class	Transformation	Raheem Sterling	Luke 33.54-62
11.Jesus is Love	Baptism, renewal	Roberto Firmino, Liverpool	2 Corinthians 5.17
12.Storms of Life	Peace	Match cancellations	Luke 8.22-25; John 14.27
13.Training Time	Kingdom	England tournaments	Revelation 21.3-5
14.True Hope	Hope	England tournaments	Hebrews 11.1; Psalm 42.11
15.Turning Point	Salvation	Comebacks; Man City	Romans 5.6
16.Hit the Showers	Sin, renewal	Bad playing conditions	Isaiah 64.6; John 13.8
17.Unexpected Call Up	God's invite	Call ups	1 Samuel 16.7
18.What are the Odds?	Christmas, prophecies	Leicester City; shocks	Micah 5.2; Isaiah 7.14
19.We All Make Mistakes...	Mistakes, forgiveness	Costly blunders	Luke 15.11-32
20.Faith in a Saviour	Hope, heroes	Superstars	Romans 10.13
21.The Price of a Play Off	Worth, sacrifice	Play offs	Matthew 13.45-46
22.Season of Hope	Hope	Man City	Jeremiah 29.11
23.Value	Value	Neymar, transfers	John 3.16
24.Remembered For What?	Legacy, who is Jesus?	Memorable players	John 3.16
25.Clean Slate	New starts, forgiveness	Tables, seasons	2 Corinthians 5.17

Here's 5 questions to prayerfully ask yourself in order to get the most out of this book:

1) Who is my **audience**?
2) **How long** do I have to speak?
3) What spiritual **theme** would I like to speak about?
4) What football reference would be **relevant** to my audience?
5) Am **I familiar** with the article enough to deliver it without reading? Rather than following by rote, these work best if the speaker is confident to improvise around the themes of the article. This is particularly important if the football references are no longer current!

Whatever your context, we'll be praying for you as you look to share Jesus by talking football!

1. I'm Available, Gaffer

Theme: God's invite

By Dan Owen

What do you do when you just can't get the attention of the manager and he doesn't see the potential in you? You love football and really think you can make a difference, but you never make the starting XI, or worse still you don't even get in the squad.

Manchester United's squad seems to have been full of these type of players recently – think Juan Mata, Donny van de Beek or Jesse Lingard. For whatever reason, these players just consistently weren't fancied by the manager.

What do you think is the biggest factor in these two players finding form? Have you ever found yourself out of favour with the manager? What did you do?

Most players have experienced both situations - raring to go but not getting the starting position and at other times playing with confidence and buzzing because of the impact you are having. Like me you may have also been through times when you've doubted your own ability and questioned the wisdom in your manager in playing you! But the key thing in all these situations is saying that you're up for it and available for selection.

Most football players I meet are pretty confident in their footballing ability, raring to get on that pitch and show the manager what they can do. I often find that when I talk to these same people about God having a role and purpose for their life, they seem less confident. It's as if they are questioning 'why would God want to use me?'. There have been times when I've invited people to church and they have responded with a desire to start coming but a sense of needing to 'sort their life out' first.

Has anyone invited you along to church? How did you feel when asked? Why didn't you go?

In a competitive environment like football you do need to earn that place on the team. Despite paying a hefty loan fee to bring Gareth Bale back to Tottenham, Jose Mourinho said: "if he wants minutes in the first team he is going to have to earn them in training, working hard."

If you were a manager what would be the key things you look for in a player to make your starting line up?

This is different to being chosen by God. God doesn't have a checklist of things you must fulfil to be good enough, He just asks you to say "I'm available gaffer".

Let Him become part of your life and change you from the inside. The Bible is full of people that didn't think they were good enough, yet God worked in and through them despite their flaws and self-doubt. A football manager will use you in his team based on your strengths, God will use your strengths, but He can also use your weaknesses for His glory.

"We now have this light shining in our hearts, but we ourselves are like fragile clay jars containing this great treasure. This makes it clear that our great power is from God, not from ourselves."

2 Corinthians 4: 7

The Bible describes our lives, even the most impressive ones simply as fragile jars of clay. It is the treasure that God puts in us that is the power to change us, those around us and our communities. He has made you the way you are, so begin owning your strengths and your weaknesses. Ask for forgiveness where it is needed and tell him you are available for selection. The book of Acts records people's responses to some ordinary fisherman that God chose to change the world.

"When they saw the courage of Peter and John and realized that they were unschooled, ordinary men, they were astonished and they took note that these men had been with Jesus."

Acts 4: 13

They were unschooled and ordinary! What's your excuse?

2. You Won't Get Sacked!

Themes:
God's value of us;
God's patience

By Alex Shoderu

Who would be a football manager? As the thin margins between defeat and victory continue to grow in financial impact, clubs seem to be more trigger-happy than ever, expecting instant return for their huge investments.

For example, in 2020 Chelsea manager Frank Lampard had been given a £200million+ investment in the squad during the summer transfer window. Therefore immediate success was required. Despite a bright start, a run of 2 wins in 8 meant Lampard was sacked by January. Do you agree with this logic, or do you think managers should be given more time to get the players working together?

Loyalty and faithfulness are important, and not just with regards to football, but just in life in general. As an Arsenal supporter, I was never a banner-holding "Wenger Out" kind of fan. Even in the last year or so before his departure when I eventually thought we needed a change, I still wanted it to be done respectfully and if possible mutually.

Thinking back to the ruthlessness of Chelsea, or more specifically, their owner Roman Abramovich, I really have a deep sense of gratitude that God does not relate to us in the same way that Abramovich relates to his managers. In the 20 years since he bought the club, Chelsea have had 14 different managers. For context, Arsenal have had just 3 in the same period! What do you make of these stats? Clearly, Chelsea value their managers less than the £200m they are willing to spend in a transfer window.

There is no doubt that God sending His Son into the world to pay for our sins came at the highest cost. It cost God much more than £200million. The Bible puts it this way:

"For you know that God paid a ransom to save you from the empty life you inherited from your ancestors. And it was not paid with mere gold or silver, which lose their value. It was the precious blood of Christ, the sinless, spotless Lamb of God."

1 Peter 1:18-19

What do you make of this verse? Have you ever thought about God paying a high price to save you?
For me it means everything. It means I am valued; it means I am known. It means I am loved. It means I don't have to earn approval. If God paid that high a price for me, I am already approved.

What I especially love about God - unlike Mr Abramovich- is that He doesn't get rid of us when we don't meet His standards. He doesn't cancel us. You won't get sacked!

"The Lord is gracious and compassionate, slow to anger, and filled with unfailing love"

Psalm 103:8

So, every time you hear of another manager getting sacked, take a minute to thank God for His unfailing love which means that if you trust him with your life, you won't ever be sacked.

3. Just a Mistake

Themes: Good Friday; how God deals with our mistakes

By Bronnie King

For all his achievements as a player and manager, Steven Gerrard will always associated with a mistake which arguably cost him, and Liverpool, their first league title in 25 years. Facing rivals Chelsea in April 2014, the Reds captain crucially slipped inside his own half, giving Demba Ba a clear run to score. Liverpool lost 2-0 and their title challenge, which looked unassailable only weeks before, crumbled.

Have you ever made a crucial mistake in a football game? How did you feel? How did your team respond?

Responding well to a mistake is crucial both in football and life in general, and Gerrard has certainly done that. But it does make you wonder... can good performance after a mistake take away what happened? Can you make up for it? What do you think?

The other day I watched a social experiment asking people: 'Is anything unforgivable'. Hearing the variety in answers was fascinating. It seemed most people wanted to be able to forgive but all agreed that there was a line. Some things were unforgivable, they believed, the main reason simply being that "you can't take it back".

When you look at your life I wonder if there are any mistakes you've made that you see as 'unforgivable'? What about in the lives of others? Should people be forgiven for their mistakes?

The thing about mistakes is that we rarely seem to view them in the right way. It's very easy to look at minor mistakes and tell yourself they're not that bad. I mean, compared to Hitler, Stalin, Mao and others, I'm a pretty good person right? I've told a white lie or said horrible things about someone else, but I've never *killed* anyone. Can my mistakes really be that bad?

Good Friday is a massive day in the Christian calendar because it's the day we remember Jesus dying on the cross. Many of us have heard the story but I wonder what it means to us? Do we realise that Good Friday isn't a disconnected series of events that happened many years ago, but it's a story that we're part of, a death that we are responsible for.

The wages of sin is death.

Romans 6.23

Sin. All sin. Not just the 'big' ones.

It's easy to compare ourselves to other people in order to make ourselves feel better, but the problem is, they're not the ones setting the standards. The almighty, *perfect* God is, and we've all fallen short. Don't compare yourselves to Hitler and see how you measure up, compare yourself to God and see how you don't. Then once you realise just how serious your mistakes are, you can start to understand the absolute necessity of the cross.

On Good Friday, Christians remember Jesus willingly giving himself up to die an excruciating death in our place, for our mistakes. If we accept that gift, we are completely and utterly forgiven, no matter what we've done. The verse in Romans 6:23 goes on to say *'For the wages of sin is death, but the free gift of God is eternal life in Christ Jesus our Lord.'* It's such a magnificent and hopeful conclusion. After reading what our sins and mistakes leave us deserving, we're left with the most glorious hope. A *free gift* from God! The most costly, life-changing gift that we contributed absolutely nothing to but just have to accept.

Good Friday is a sombre day where I am reminded of just how much my sin cost Jesus. But it's a day that's so far from hopeless because I know the story has a happy ending. Three days after Jesus' death, we read the miraculous account of Jesus' resurrection. In Matthew 28:5-6 some women go to Jesus' tomb and find the stone covering the entrance rolled away. An angel tells them *"Do not be afraid, for I know that you are looking for Jesus, who was crucified. He is not here; He has risen, just as He said! Come, see the place where He lay'.*

Jesus' sacrifice was accepted by God and he didn't stay in the grave. He fully defeated death and rose again, triumphant and exalted into the position he rightly deserved. On Easter Sunday that's what we celebrate and now we're free to see our mistakes in the right light. They're serious, they matter, but there is nothing we can't be forgiven for if we have accepted Jesus' free gift. *Absolutely nothing.*

Do you know that your sin is serious?
Do you know that you can be forgiven?
Have you accepted Jesus' sacrifice on the cross or are you going to pay it yourself?

4. Who Would You Pick?

Themes: Grace

By Tom Woodbridge

One of the hardest parts of an international manager's job has to be choosing their final squad for major tournaments. The European Championships in 2021 presented England manager Gareth Southgate with a huge dilemma at right back, with no less than four players all vying for a place. Would Walker and Trippier offer England enough options? Is Reece James experienced enough? Can Trent Alexander-Arnold's defensive weaknesses be overlooked because of his outstanding attacking threat? Everyone seemed to have an opinion on each player's strengths and weaknesses.

Some people have a similar attitude when it comes to God, am I good enough to get picked? We can even find ourselves using the same kind of criteria: what are my strengths? What are my weaknesses? What can I offer God? Am I up to his standard? And yet the astonishing thing is that God doesn't work that way!

In nearly every sphere of life, including football, it is about proving yourself. You've got to be good enough to make it. Prove it to your manager, prove it to your teammates, prove it to the fans. Are you good enough? But with God, that's not how it works!

Do you ever ask yourself these kind of questions?

Listen to these words from the Bible:

> *For it is by grace you have been saved, through faith - and this is not from yourselves, it is the gift of God - not by works, so that no one can boast.*
>
> Ephesians 2.8-9

Do you see what the writer, the Apostle Paul says? God doesn't save us by our works. We don't prove how good we are to God by what we do. No, we are saved only by grace! God sent His Son, Jesus to die in our place, not because we deserve it, but simply because He loves us. It's His choice, His motivation to save us. It's nothing about what we have done or can do to be good enough.

So if the pressure's on to perform to earn your place, or keep your place, remember that with God, it's not about your performance, it's all about His grace to you through Jesus Christ that saves you.

5. Spiritually Skint or God's Grace?

Themes: Grace; God's Kingdom

Written by Sam Gibb

The European Super League may already seem like old news, one of many "did that really happen?" moments of 2021. But if I have any understanding of football, then the ESL is a beast that has retreated back into its (ridiculously expensive) cave but will in time shed its skin, change enough of its spots, and come back again fighting – as big and ugly as ever. And one day, it will probably win.

What about you? Do you think we've really seen the last of the ESL?

The reason is this: money talks. And when it comes to football, those with the biggest wallets always seem to have the last word. In so much of sport and so much of life this is the case. Those with thrive and those without barely survive. Money and power rule. And everyone else just follows along.

But amazingly it won't always be like this, and even now it doesn't have to be– there is a different way to live. Jesus, in his top-notch-better-than-anything-on-Netflix Sermon on the Mount speaks about a better world in these life changing upside-down words:

Blessed are the poor in spirit,
for theirs is the kingdom of heaven
Blessed are the meek,
for they will inherit the earth.

Matthew 5:4-5

When it comes to Jesus, it is the spiritually skint who receive a kingdom! It is the meek, not the powerful, who inherit the whole earth! So, even if the European Super League does eventually win, it will be temporary. God is reserving all things for the humble not the proud, for the skint not the rich.

But 'meek' and 'poor in spirit' isn't really talking about what's in our wallets, but what's in our hearts - and that is far more important. The 'poor in spirit' are those who know that they bring nothing to the party themselves. Unlike the Super League 12, who all had the right size bank accounts to get a seat at the table, those who are 'spiritually skint' realise that they can give nothing to God to receive his love. No good-works bank balance or religious currency can buy access to the kingdom of Heaven. The only way into this kingdom, the eternal kingdom, is not believing you are good enough but realising you are bad enough and yet, God's grace is enough.

Jesus, on the cross, paid the price for you. So put away your wallet and put your faith in him!

Do you try to get into the kingdom of Heaven with your own good works?
Why won't this work?
What is the only way in?

6. Great Save

Theme: salvation

By Martin Bateman

Who is the best goalkeeper in the Premier League? What is the best save you have ever seen?

Goalkeeping is one of the hardest positions. Many teams struggle to find a reliable keeper as it is such an important position. Outfield players can mess up and be bailed out by their teammates, but if a keeper makes a mistake then a goal is likely.

In life we all make mistakes and errors that can cost us, and those around us. But if Jesus is your goalkeeper he can be fully relied upon as he never makes mistakes. In fact, he deals with our mistakes if we let Him!

"If you declare with your mouth, "Jesus is Lord," and believe in your heart that God raised him from the dead, you will be saved. For it is with your heart that you believe and are justified, and it is with your mouth that you profess your faith and are saved .Everyone who calls on the name of the Lord will be saved".

Romans 10:9-13

We all can be saved from our mistakes if we declare Jesus is Lord. What difference would it make for you if you had a safe pair of hands in goal behind you?

7. Hope for the Future

Themes: transformation

By Mark Williams

In 2021, the completion of a take-over bid at Newcastle led by a Saudi Arabia based consortium made them the richest clubs in the world. It's not the first time we've seen this kind of high-profile take-over - Chelsea, Man City and PSG have all benefited from wealthy new owners in the past.

What do you think about big money takeovers in football?

Big money takeovers like this often transform the mood around the club over-night, from one of frustration about the lack of ambition to one of huge hope and optimism. A team that was seemingly going nowhere, now has a realistic chance to become one of the top clubs in the country, if not Europe.

As a Christian, I see this as a picture of an immediate transformation in my life and in the lives of countless others who have decided to follow Jesus. The Bible puts it like this:

"All of us also lived among them at one time, gratifying the cravings of our flesh and following its desires and thoughts. Like the rest, we were by nature deserving of wrath. But because of his great love for us, God, who is rich in mercy, made us alive with Christ even when we were dead in transgressions - it is by grace you have been saved." (Ephesians 2:3-5)

The moment that I recognised that I'm not a perfect person but that I wanted to follow Jesus, in a spiritual sense my future changed from one that looked bleak and deserving of God's wrath, to one of hope and optimism knowing that I'd been made right with God. In making that choice, I didn't instantly become a perfect person, and I'm still not, but I set out on a journey of faith.

If we're honest, Newcastle haven't instantly transformed into the perfect club at the pinnacle of European football either. There is plenty of hard work ahead if the new owners are going to take the club from where they are to one that is seriously and consistently challenging for honours.

If they are to follow in the footsteps of Man City, who were taken over by billionaire owners in 2008, I would argue that the Newcastle need to change from the inside, out. They will need to establish a new mind-set and lay out clear goals on everything from the infrastructure of the club to marketing, player recruitment and their academy. It will take time, but it's do-able.

In my own life, since I made the decision to follow Jesus I know that I have been changing from the inside out. I may be a work in progress but I know that God is working in my life and he's in it for the long-haul. He's promised to carry on working until his work in me is finished.

Are you needing a transformation in your life?

Would you be willing to be changed from the inside out?

God is ready and waiting to invest in your life and bring you hope for the future.

8. Writing on the Wall...

Themes: sin and salvation

By Josh Fortune

Being a football manager can be a tough job. Google 'Man Utd managers before and after photos' and see the evidence for yourself. It's very hard to hide! As a manager you will have to face the cameras, the boos from supporters, and the media articles calling for your head after a string of bad results. Many managers will know that their time is up before they even get the fateful call from the owner. You can tell by their body language as they walk off the pitch after yet another defeat. They know as well as we do - the writing is on the wall, their time is up.

Have you ever been in a situation where you know the 'writing is on the wall'?

That phrase comes from the Bible. In Daniel chapter 5, the Babylonian king Belshazzar is throwing a big party.

Full of wine, he starts to disrespect God! Suddenly a great hand starts writing on the wall: *'MENE, MENE, TEKEL, PARSIN.'*

Summoning the prophet Daniel, the shaken king hears that God is giving him a clear message: The days of his reign have been numbered. He has been found wanting. His kingdom will be removed. That very night, Belshazzar's kingdom fell - and he lost his life. Belshazzar, like many football managers after a bad string of results, was found out and removed.

We may not be kings or even football managers, but we all need to learn the lesson of the writing on the wall. Everything we have ever said, thought, and done is known by God. In His sight we are ALL found wanting.

All have sinned and fallen short of the glory of God

Romans 3.23'

Jesus sums up the requirements of the law in two commands: Love God with all our being, and love other people like we love ourselves. How many of us have kept these both perfectly? Not even close! And so we have a problem. We are not facing the boos from fans, or the loss of our jobs - no, we are facing something far worse: the justice of a Holy God.

What hope do we have? A substitution.

Managers are often criticised for their substitution choices, making the wrong changes too early or too late. However, God made the perfect swap when He sent His only Son, Jesus Christ, to be born into this world - live the perfect life we couldn't - and die on the cross for the sins of His people. By trusting in Christ, we can be saved from the writing on the wall.

You could add up ALL the bad results that sacked managers this year have had, but they don't even come close to the wrong things I have done in my life.

I am weighed, measured, and found wanting.

Jesus was weighed, measured, and found to be perfect. Trust in Him today, follow Him with all your heart and then - unlike many in the managerial hot seat this season - you will have nothing to fear in the future.

Have you accepted Jesus as your substitute?

9. The God of Second Chances

Themes: injustice; salvation

By Rob Taylor

Few will easily forget the harrowing scenes that took place on Saturday 12th June 2021, when Christian Eriksen suddenly collapsed with heart failure, 43 minutes into Denmark's Euro 2021 match with neighbours Finland. Shielded by Eriksen's encircled team mates, doctors performed CPR on the Inter Milan midfielder in front of a stunned Copenhagen crowd. Prayers were offered up on the pitch, in the stands and across the world.

Where were you when Eriksen collapsed?
What are your memories of the event?

Mercifully, Eriksen has now made a full recovery and has now been fitted with an ICD pacemaker to reduce future risks. Thanks to the skill of the doctors on the pitch and the wonders of modern medicine, the Dane has been given a second chance at life.

Continuing his career, however, has proven more complicated. Serie A regulations state that no player fitted with an ICD can play, leaving Eriksen in a similar position to Fabrice Muamba, who was eventually forced to retire after his horrific on-field collapse in 2012. With his Inter contract cancelled, the former Tottenham player's retirement seemed sadly inevitable, despite his valiant efforts to prove his fitness. This must have felt supremely unfair to Eriksen, having devoted his life to nurturing his talents, rising to spearhead Inter's title win in his only season at the San Siro.

Have you experienced a time when life seemed unfair? Have you seen your own hard work wiped out by unexpected life events? How did it feel?

Then we arrive at an unexpected twist. A discrepancy between Serie A and Premier League regulations was discovered, and with the January 2022 transfer window only hours from shutting, it was announced that Eriksen would sensationally sign for Premier League side Brentford.

"We have taken an unbelievable opportunity to bring a world-class player to Brentford," said Bees boss Thomas

Frank. When all seemed lost, Eriksen's career had been given an unforeseen opportunity to reignite.

Unfortunately, we live in a world that is unfair. Like Christian Eriksen experienced, sometimes events entirely out of our control mean that our best-laid plans are torn up, and our future is thrown into turmoil. The Bible reflects this theme too. While the likes of Moses, Jonah and David made big mistakes and had to live with the consequences, spare a thought for Daniel, who by no mistake of his own, was exiled to Babylon along with the rest of Israel. Daniel's future must have seemed very bleak at this point.

But like Brentford offering Eriksen a second chance out-of-the-blue, so too did God offer Daniel (and Israel) a second chance at life. What we discover when we examine this theme further is that this is in God's very nature.

Psalm 86 declares that God is: *'merciful and gracious, slow to anger and abounding in steadfast love and faithfulness.'* If we trust our lives in the hands of God, no redemption is too hard.

At the very start if his ministry, Jesus quoted the book of Isaiah when he declared that:

> *"The Spirit of the Lord is on me, because He has anointed me to proclaim good news to the poor. He has sent me to proclaim freedom for the prisoners and recovery of sight for the blind, to set the oppressed free, to proclaim the year of the Lord's favour".*
>
> *Luke 4.18-19*

Jesus' ministry was marked by fresh starts and second chances. He redeemed the outcasts, the liars, the stricken and those forgotten by society. We see in Jesus' words and actions the unfaltering power of God's redemption. So whatever life has thrown at you, and however far you feel you've fallen, remember that God is the God of second chances, and nothing is beyond His redemptive power.

Where do you need God's redemptive power in your life today?

10. World Class

Theme: Transformation

By Jonathan Blair

Many football pundits now say that Raheem Sterling has become truly world class. Consistently brilliant performances for England and Man City have made him one of the first names on the team sheet. However, it wasn't too long ago though that things were very different. Many people were calling for him to be dropped in the World Cup as he was on a dreadful run of having not scored for his country. Now, he just can't stop scoring.

So how has he turned around his career? Do you think he is world class?

When we look at the stories from Jesus' time we see a group of guys who journeyed with Jesus. However, they were far from being world class, in fact when Jesus needed his mates, his mates left him.

Arresting Jesus, they marched him off and took him into the house of the Chief Priest. Peter followed, but at a safe distance. In the middle of the courtyard some people had started a fire and were sitting around it, trying to keep warm. One of the serving maids sitting at the fire noticed him, then took a second look and said, "This man was with Jesus!"

Peter denied it, "Woman, I don't even know him."

A short time later, someone else noticed him and said, "You're one of them." But Perter denied it again.

About an hour later, someone else spoke up, really adamant: "He's got to have been with him! He's got 'Galilean' written all over him."

Peter said, "I don't know what you're talking about." AT that very moment, a rooster crowed. Jesus turned and looked at Peter. Peter remembered what Jesus had said to him: "Before the rooster crows, you will deny me three times." He went out and cried bitterly.

Luke 22.54-62

Jesus was arrested. He needed his mates to stand with him. Instead they deserted him. When asked if he knew Jesus, Peter wouldn't even admit it to a young girl.

On any scale Peter was a failure, fraud and a rubbish mate. However, if we look a couple of months ahead at the day of Pentecost you see Peter sharing to thousands about who Jesus was. He was sharing in the open air so everyone could hear him. He was now not ashamed of who heard, and what he was saying. He was nailing his colours to the mast, he was a follower of Jesus and now he wanted the world to know.

In the space of few months he had gone from failure to formidable. What changed?

After rising from the dead on Easter Day, Jesus met Peter again. He restored Peter, he didn't condemn him. He also shared with Peter his purpose, to be the rock upon which the church is built. Jesus gave purpose, He gave direction, and He showed he cared for Peter. Peter was a transformed man, and became a person that the church was built upon.

When everyone was blaming Raheem Sterling for England not winning the World Cup, Pep Guardiola texted him and said, “You’re my man”. I am not sure why Raheem has gone from strength to strength, but it helps to know you have a manager that cares, believes, and has shown you how his abilities can fit within the team.

Today, where are you at? Do you feel you are fulfilling your potential or is there more to come from you? Who are you looking towards to help you become world class? As Peter found, there’s no better man-manager available than Jesus, if you put him in charge of your life.

11. Jesus is Love

Themes: baptism, renewal

By Stephen Read

Have you seen the clip from a few years ago of Roberto Firmino getting baptised? In the video is another Liverpool player, goalkeeper Alisson Becker, and in the crowd was their teammate, Fabinho.

On Instagram, Firmino said, *"I gave you my failures and the victories I will give you too. My greatest title is Your Love Jesus! Therefore, if anyone is in Christ, he is a new creation. The old things have passed away; behold, new things have come"! New time."*

In the video, before he was baptised he says: *"Jesus is love. (There is) no explanation. Just believe it. Just believe and feel the Holy Spirit"*

What do think of Firmino being baptised? What do think when he says, "Jesus is Love"?

In *1 John 4:8* it says, *"God is love."* In His essential nature, God is love. Everything about Him is love. God longs to love you and be a father to you. He wants you to take all your failures, worries, concerns, angers, hurts, joy, happiness and victories to Him. In and through everything, He wants to be with you, and through Jesus' death and resurrection He wants you to spend eternity with Him.

Firmino quotes the Bible:

> *"Therefore, if anyone is in Christ, he is a new creation; the old has gone, the new has come!"*
>
> *2 Corinthians 5.17*

If you believe that Jesus died and was resurrected on the cross for you, then you can be completely forgiven. You will be made new and all your past wrongs forgiven and God will be in your heart where you can know his love and presence.

Would you like to become a new creation today?

12. Storms of Life

Theme: peace

By Matt Round

In today's game, it's extremely rare to see a Premier League fixture cancelled due to weather conditions. It's so rare in fact, that only 3 Premier League fixtures have been cancelled in the last 6 years. Though it's much more common to see fixture cancellations the further down the leagues you go, there is nothing more frustrating than gearing up for game day, to then have it called off because the pitch is under 1ft of water.

Have you ever had a last minute fixture cancellation due to weather conditions?
How does it make you feel when you are told the games off?

Playing in the local Saturday league, fixture cancellations can sometimes seem to be an alien concept. It doesn't matter if there's a storm, some fixtures just must be played and it is how we cope in the conditions that determines the result. What's the worst conditions you have ever had to play in?

Just like a football match can be impacted by a physical storm, we too can be impacted by the storms of life.

In the Bible we read how Jesus and the disciples encountered a storm whilst sailing across Lake Galilee:

One day Jesus said to his disciples, "Let's go over to the other side of the lake." So they got into a boat and set out. As they sailed, he fell asleep. A storm came down on the lake, so that the boat was being swamped, and they were in great danger. The disciples went and woke him, saying, "Master, Master, we're going to drown!"

He got up and rebuked the wind and raging waters; the storm subsided, and all was calm. "Where is your faith?" he asked his disciples.

In fear and amazement they asked one another, "Who is this man? He commands even the winds and the water, and they obey him."

Luke 8.22-25

Whilst the disciples entered panic mode fearing the worst, Jesus was calmly sleeping. That's a strange thing to do whilst in the middle of a storm. How would you have reacted if you were one of the disciples?

After being woken by his frenzied friends, Jesus spoke to the wind and waves: *"Quiet! Be still"*. At the sound of his voice, all became calm! WOW! Just think about that for a moment.

Jesus has the power to calm the physical storms - but he also has the power to bring calm to us in the storms of life; He tells us He gives us His peace.

> *"Peace I leave with you; my peace I give you. I do not give to you as the world gives. Do not let your hearts be troubled and do not be afraid."*
>
> *John 14:27*

What storms of life are you currently going through that need Jesus' calming power?
If you could have peace in any situation right now, what would it be?

13. Training Time

Themes: God's Kingdom

By Rob Taylor

In the weeks before a major international football tournament you can guarantee two things:

1) unrealistic media hype around England's chances; and
2) regular access inside the team's training camp.

This is always fascinating, as two dozen pampered athletes adapt to the monotonous regime of a month shut away from home comforts, friends and family.

In the past, England managers have struggled to strike the right balance in the atmosphere they create within the camp. In 2006, England's Baden-Baden hotel was described as a "holiday camp" and a "circus", with the lack of discipline being blamed for England's under-performance. Adversely, Fabio Capello was so strict with his group in 2010 (players were isolated from spouses and even denied everyday luxuries like butter on their toast) that there was open criticism of a stifling environment that felt like a boarding school.

In both cases, the wrong regime created the wrong results. What went wrong at past World Cups inside the England training camps?

Have you ever experienced an environment that was so flawed or toxic that you couldn't be yourself, or produce your best work? Have you longed for something better?

Jesus repeatedly began his parables by saying, "this is what the kingdom of God is like," or, "what shall we say the kingdom of God is like?" In other words, what is life like under God's regime? What can we expect in God's training camp, when we let Him be in charge of our lives, our communities and our world?

The Bible describes a time to come when God will make all things new, when:

> *He will wipe away every tear from their eyes, and there will be no more death or mourning or crying or pain.*
>
> *Revelation 21.3-5*

For those tired of death, disease and injustice, we have a sure hope that in God's regime, these things will be gone for ever.

However, the Christian faith is not a pie-in-the-sky dream. Most of Jesus' teachings focused on establishing God's Kingdom on earth *now*. Even His most famous prayer asks for "your kingdom come, your will be done, on earth as it is in heaven." (Matthew 6.10).

The real kicker is that *we* are tasked with working to establish God's Kingdom here on earth. Jesus' life, death and resurrection were a gloriously defiant declaration of war against sin, death and injustice. But it is us who continue the fight in His name and through His power.

Every act of loving service, every forgiving word, every life turned around and realigned with God's way is a powerful weapon in the battle, as we await the day when God's regime is forever established, full of love, peace and joy.

Are you part of God's Kingdom?

14. True hope?

Themes: Hope

By Josh Fortune

I love the group stages of international football. Hope abounds everywhere you look. Fans across the world wonder whether this is their moment and, for one team, it will be.

After having fallen in love with England after watching World Cup '98 (and THAT Argentina match...), each tournament has pretty much the same cycle for me:

- Tournament build up - I tell myself there is no hope of winning at all (I do this to try and guard my heart. It never works.)

- Group stages - Despite England generally playing fairly tepid football, hope begins to grow (after all, Portugal won

Euro 2016 despite having a fairly shocking tournament, right?)

- Last 16 - England scrape one - maybe two wins - hope is alive! Is it coming home?

- Quarter/Semi Finals - Oh. Never mind.

The problem with hope in football is that you cannot base the hope on anything solid. Even the best-playing, most confident teams can suffer a shocking loss in a final against the run of play (we've seen plenty of those in recent years!). Therefore, the only hope that even the most avid fan can cling to is not guaranteed or built on anything solid. It is optimistic yet wishful thinking.

We've all seen cameras zooming in on faces of distraught fans whose hopes have been dashed. How many times have your sporting hopes been let down?

The Bible speaks a lot about hope, but not the sort of 'I *hope* England win' type of hope. Biblical hope is not wishful thinking. Biblical hope is not built on creaky foundations. Biblical hope is inextricably linked with faith.

'Now faith is confidence in what we hope for and assurance about what we do not see.'

Hebrews 11.1

Confidence and assurance in what we have not yet seen or reached yet. Football fans may claim to be confident - but nobody can be absolutely assured of their teams' chances. Not so the Christian! Even though we have neither seen God nor the place He has prepared for us when we go to be with Him, we can look forward with confidence and expectant assurance: God's promises are true, and we can trust in Him with full hope!

Do you know the sure hope of a future with Christ?

When England get knocked out of tournaments, I'm a bit sad - but I'm not devastated, because I have something better to hope for. My hope transcends anything that people hope for in this world - because my hope is found in God.

Why, my soul, are you downcast?
Why so disturbed within me?
Put your hope in God,
for I will yet praise him,
my Saviour and my God.

Psalm 42.11

15. Turning Point

Theme: salvation

By Mark Williams

Throughout any football season, there will be countless moments that change the fortunes of any given team. Sometimes it comes down to the finest of margins, a costly mistake or a moment of sheer brilliance. Any of these things could swing a game, or even the outcome of a season, in a team's favour.

Can you think of any big moments in recent seasons that have changed the outcome for the team you support or play for? How did these moments leave you feeling?

Part of the beauty of football is that it can be so unpredictable and we never know what's going happen. Every now and then, there are those moments we later recognise as turning points for our team.

As a Man City fan, I remember witnessing one of the biggest turning points in the club's history at the old Wembley way back in May 1999. 2-0 down on 89 minutes having conceded both goals in the last 10 minutes of the game, in the stands I just wanted the game to be over so the pain would stop. Yet 5 minutes later, with the game somehow 2-2 the pain was gone, unbelievable relief and joy in its place. I've rarely been part of such wild celebrations as when the equaliser went in. Leaping around, screaming and shouting, hugging random strangers! I even got bruises on both shins from bashing them on the wooden seat in front as I was celebrating. I didn't care and City went on to clinch promotion. One of the commentators in the studio stated that City had "come back from the dead". That's how it felt in the stands. It's hard to imagine that without that moment, without that equalising goal at just the right time, City would be where they are now.

I love thinking back to that moment as it reminds me of the biggest turning point of all time. In the Bible, Paul reminds us in his letter to the early church in Rome that:

> *"At just the right time, when we were still powerless, Christ died for the ungodly."*
>
> *Romans 5:6*

In the stands, as supporters, we're powerless to affect the game – we can only watch as events unfold. As people we're all guilty of sin as none of us are perfect. That sin carries with it eternal consequences, not to mention pain and guilt during our lifetimes. We're powerless to make things right with God and there is nothing we can do to earn our way back to Him, to be deserving of His forgiveness. Yet at just the right moment, Jesus provided that turning point for all of mankind when he chose to die in our place and then three days later literally came back from the dead. By choosing to put our faith in Him and receive his free gift of forgiveness, the pain, guilt and consequences of our sin our gone, dealt with, relief and joy left in its place.

Do you need to know that turning point in your life today?

16. Hit The Showers

Themes: sin, renewal

By Dan Owen

As someone who loves playing football there is only ever one point in the year my love of playing the beautiful game will dip - the depths of winter! I always find it hard to motivate myself to scrape the ice of the car, drive to a freezing cold changing room (that if it does have a heater is the size of a travel hairdryer and probably doesn't work anyway), the pitch is a semi-defrosted bog and your touch is dreadful because you've lost all feeling in your feet! Beautiful is the last word you would associate with amateur football in January, especially as you walk off the pitch coated in mud.

What are the worst conditions you've played in? How bad do conditions have to be for you to hope the game gets called off?

There was one saving grace about playing in awful weather at our home ground in Bolton - it had the best showers! They were hot, powerful, plenty to go round and no matter how cold, bloody and muddy you were from the winter battle you could wash it all away and get warm before going to the pub!

Can you imagine if a player never washed after a game, nor when they got home or the following day? They probably wouldn't be invited out post-match! It's impossible to get through a game without being dirty and smelly, and it's the same with life. It's impossible to get through without making bad choices, offending others and worst of all God.

'All of us have become like one who is unclean, and all our righteous acts are like filthy rags.'

Isaiah 64:6

The stains of all the wrong things we do in life are called sin. They aren't as easy to see as the mud and sweat following a football match, but the consequences are far more severe. They cause guilt, shame, damaged relationships and also a separation from God himself.

What makes Christianity unique is that Jesus has the authority to forgive sin. All other religions point to ways of trying to get rid of the sin whereas Jesus points to his own chest and says come to me and I'll make you clean.

Jesus answered, "Unless I wash you, you have no part with me."

John 13:8

Would you have a bath before getting in the shower? Of course not, the purpose of it is to get clean. It's the same with giving your life to Jesus. You don't need to sort yourself out, deal with that habit or clean up your ways first. He gave his life on the cross to pay the price for your sin.

Are you concerned by your spiritual hygiene?
Do you know what it is like to feel clean spiritually?

Jesus invites you to bring all your sin, guilt and shame to him and he'll wash it away.

17. Unexpected call-up

Theme: God's call

Written by Mark Chester

Have you ever dreamed of pulling on your favourite team's colours and scoring the winner on your debut, in front of a full stadium? Sadly, very few of us get the chance but it doesn't stop us imagining what it must feel like, and sometimes we hope for it long after there is any chance of it happening. There is a famous interview with a middle-aged Liverpool fan in which he says he can make himself go to sleep at night thinking of the roar of the Kop and fancying himself thundering down the wing with his stomach hanging over his shorts and scoring a vital goal.

Imagine that one day you receive a phone call and are surprised to hear the manager of the national team on the other end of the line. You are even more surprised to hear that he has selected you to play for the national team. You arrive at training and discover that the other men who have been called up include a 25-year-old who has not played since he was in his Cub Scout team and a pair of brothers who have never even owned a football. It's ridiculous, isn't it? It makes no sense.

How would you feel if you did receive an unexpected call-up?

When Jesus selected his team - the men who would be responsible for conveying his message to the world - he did not make the obvious choices. He did not pick religious leaders and preachers, experts in theology and experienced communicators, to be his disciples. Instead he chose fisherman and a hated tax collector, people who were apparently as unsuitable for the task as you and I would be for representing their country at football. Clearly, Jesus had a different way of looking at people and assessing their potential.

How would you choose members of a team? What criteria would you use?

When Samuel was sent by God to appoint the person who would become king over Israel, he was about to choose the wrong person. God said to him:

'The Lord does not look at the things people look at. People look at the outward appearance, but the Lord looks at the heart.'

1 Samuel 16:7

So don't be constrained by your own feelings of inadequacy, doubts about how you look or lack of self-confidence. There is a place for you on God's team.

18. What are the odds?

Themes: Christmas; Jesus fulfilling unlikely prophecies

Written by Gareth Haddow

Few will easily forget Leicester City's amazing Premier League win in 2016. After only just surviving relegation the season before, not even the most optimistic Leicester fan would have even considered them title contenders before the season's start. In fact, you could have got odds of 5000-1 on them lifting the trophy – far longer odds than such unlikely events as the finding of the Loch Ness Monster, or Simon Cowell being elected Prime Minister. But from nowhere, the largely unheard of Jamie Vardy, Riyad Mahrez and N'Golo Kante fired the Foxes to their first ever league title win, leaving the expensively-assembled squads of Liverpool, Man City and Tottenham behind.

The odds of Leicester winning the Premier League were very great. Likewise, the odds of all the prophesies about Jesus coming true were very great. Written hundreds of years before, The Old Testament includes over 300 predictions about Jesus, around 48 . The odds of 8 of these prophecies coming true are 1 in 100,000,000,000,000,000. The odds of 48 prophecies being fulfilled? 1 chance in 10 to the 157th power. Yet *every single one* of the 300+ prophecies was fulfilled!

Some of the prophecies included:

Jesus would be born in Bethlehem - Micah 5:2
Jesus would be born of a virgin - Isaiah 7:14
Jesus would come from the tribe of Judah - Genesis 49:10
Jesus would be declared the son of God - Psalm 2:7

Why do you think there were so many specific predictions?
Have we stopped to think about the true meaning of Christmas?
Do you believe the Christmas story and how has it changed your life?

19. We All Make Mistakes...

Themes:
mistakes,
forgiveness

Written by Matt Round

Have you ever made a bad mistake whilst playing football? I remember playing in goal and making a very costly mistake. The opposition attacker broke free from our defence, and realising I was out of position I started to run backwards. That was my mistake! Saturday amateur football doesn't have the luxury of flat surfaces, and whilst trying to get in position I managed to trip myself up - stumbled over - only to watch the attackers shot bounce through my legs into an open net - whilst I sat in a heap on the floor. We lost that game 1-0.

How do you respond to mistakes made by yourself?
How do you respond to mistakes made by your teammates?

After the goalkeeping fiasco I swore to myself I would never play in goal again! I didn't want to put myself through that humiliation or let the team down again. And I'm sure some of my teammates felt the same. We all react in different ways when both we and/or our teammates make a mistake.

The Bible says we ALL make mistakes, we all get things wrong and we all mess up – so at least we aren't on our own in this! Jesus told a story of a son who wanted to live life his own way.

The son asked for his inheritance early and on receiving it, left the family home for a new country. Enjoying life to the full, it wasn't long before the money was no more and the son was left without food, without shelter or any friends. Reaching rock bottom, the son knew he had made a mistake and was reminded that even the workers of his father's house had food and shelter. So, the next day he set off back home – hoping his dad would allow him to live & work as a worker on his farm.

On returning to the family home, the father saw from a distance his son and without hesitation ran to him, hugged him and celebrated his return!

Luke 15.11-32

What stands out for you in this story?

When we make mistakes in life, and let's face it we all do, we can often feel at rock bottom. We feel that we have let ourselves, friends and family down. It can be hard to recover. The father in this story represents God. The good news is that God welcomes His children who have made mistakes, messed up and feel like they have hit rock bottom. He's a forgiving father - who loves His children!

No matter what mistakes you may have made in life, God loves you, cares for you and is willing you to come home to Him. He forgives our mistakes - and celebrates our return!

20. Faith in a Saviour

Themes: hope; heroes

Written by Joe Lowther

Who are your heroes in football?

How heroes are built, only to vanish. All our clubs have them. Dalglish at Liverpool, Cantona at Manchester United, Shearer at Newcastle, Henry at Arsenal, Le Tissier at Southampton. One minute they are there, the next they are gone.

How do we survive these changes of such highs and such lows as football fans? The elation... and then it disappears. People say it's what keeps us watching but that's wrong - nobody in their right mind believes that - it's the glory of winning that people want not defeat. We want what Kevin Keegan himself was called at Newcastle - the Messiah. Sadly for all the great memories and glorious football he delivered, it ended and failed to even produce even one trophy.

Henry, Cantona, Keegan - we all want a saviour who provides the joy we crave, which doesn't stop. Even Sir Alex Ferguson's reign ended and look at the shadow of their former selves United now are.

To find true glory, deep joy and un-ending peace there is only one hero we can turn too. One saviour. One Lord. He outlives footballs trials and outperforms where others struggle. He prepares a Kingdom which is paved with gold and will reign in glorious majesty for ever. His name is Jesus Christ. He is answer for all our questions, hopes and dreams.

Which Saviour will you pick?

Anyone who calls on the name of the Lord will be saved.

Romans 10.13

21. The Price of a Playoff

Written by James Yielder

Theme: God's worth

This time of year is known for playoff football. 46 league games coming down to a one-off match where the winner takes all. Form and money goes out the window and all hopes of promotion rest on the performance on the day. What is the greatest playoff moment you have seen?

The single match can be the difference in millions of pounds. With the Championship playoff final last year being worth a reported £200million to the team that won.

Aside from the money there will also be a number of jobs on the line depending on who gets promoted and who stays down. With the value of being promoted so high the demand and pressure on the players and coaches are higher as well.

The allure of promotion also leads to many teams spending a lot of money throughout the year in order to try and secure promotion. However, money can't always guarantee success in football. The more money your team spends without achieving promotion, the less financially stable your team often becomes and soon your team can move from one looking to get promoted to one fighting for survival, as the financial repercussions hit.

As a fan would you want your team to put its financial stability at risk for the gamble of promotion?

In Matthew 13.45-46 Jesus tells a story about a merchant who found a pearl that he really wanted. His desire for this pearl was so much that he was willing to sell all his possessions in order to buy it. Is there something of great value that you really want and would be willing to sacrifice a lot for?

At the start of this story we are told that the pearl represents the kingdom of heaven - the value and reward of heaven is so great that it should be more important than anything and everything we have now. Like a team pushing for playoff glory there is a risk, but the reward is infinitely worth it.

Jesus says that He is 'The Way' (John 14) and that no one gets to heaven except through Him. The offer is there for all of us to be in relationship with Jesus and as a result get to heaven; do you want to?

22. Season of Hope

Themes: hope

Written by Ben Cutting

Football. A game that brings out the best and worst in us! It's a love-hate relationship. Most of us know what it feels like for our team to go through a tough time. A season of defeat and difficulty. For some of us that's a reality we know all too well and there doesn't seem to be an end. But we carry on watching, we carry on playing in the hope that one day we will reach a place of victory and good times will come to the club we love.

Take Manchester City for example, after years of dashed hopes and disappointments, the good times are well and truly here. One of my best friends is a lifelong City fan and I think he is still pinching himself in regards to the rise of his club! Not all of us will have Man City moments with our teams but we will experience joy and good times just around the corner. Isn't that why we watch football?

I asked my friend Josh (the lifelong City fan) if all those horrible times with Man City were worth it now. I asked him if he had to go through more times of hard ache to experience more joy at the end of it would he. Would he watch his side struggle again knowing that the good times would come? He said ABSOLUTELY!

Life can often seem like a constant season of defeat or difficulties. One loss after another. How many times have we experienced playing well and then losing a game to a last minute winner? The same applies for the game of life doesn't it? Other times it seems like we need to park the bus and just take attack after attack and we can't seem to stop things from going wrong. But like in football as in life, we have a joy and a hope in what is to come.

The hope of heaven is a reality for Christians. God's promise of the life to come is one of victory. It's going to be like being a Man City fan and experiencing that moment when Aguero scored the last minute winner against QPR to win the league title, but the good news for us is we don't have to support Man City. Our moment applies to those who have faith is Christ. And our moment isn't forgotten the following year. It is it's never going to end.

Hold on, hope is on its way.

For I know the plans I have for you, declares the Lord, plans to prosper you and not to harm you, plans to give you hope and a future.

Jeremiah 29.11

23. Value

Theme: value

Written by Lucas Heubeck

When Neymar moved from Barcelona to PSG in August 2017 he became the world's most expensive signing. The French side had to part with an eye-watering £200m to trigger his release clause. This huge amount has not yet come close to being matched.

What is value to you? How much do you think you're worth as a footballer? What is your value as a person? Our value can be influenced by circumstances, our past or even what others say about us.

It is great to know that God sees enormous value in everyone, regardless of who you are. If you take a £10 note, we all know that the value of it is £10, no more and no less. If you shout at it as loud as you can it is still worth £10! If you screw it up, stamp on it or make a cut in it, it would still be worth £10!

Nothing can change your value in God's eyes. You are more worth more than what you can put a price to, because you are loved by our heavenly Father. God evaluates everyone the same, he loves everyone the same and died for everyone.

"For God so loved the world, that He gave His only begotten Son, that whoever believes in Him shall not perish, but have eternal life."

John 3.16

So next time you are feeling low or worthless remember that God paid the ultimate price for you in sending His son to die for you. That makes you as valuable as Neymar!

24. Remembered for What?

Themes: legacy; who is Jesus?

By Mark Blythe

Which footballers, who no longer play, do you remember for good reasons?

I can think of Bobby Robson, Gary Lineker, Bobby Moore, Linvoy Primus – any others? Those guys had good reputations because of their characters as well as their footballing abilities.

Which footballers do you remember for not so good reasons? Luis Suarez, Maradona, Thierry Henry, Ched Evans, Ron Chopper Harris, Eric Cantona. What a shame that these guys with amazing footballing talents can be remembered more for the 'not so good' things they have done rather than their abilities. Character is remembered for longer than ability.

What do you think you will be remembered for?
What would you like to be remembered for?

Jesus lived about 2000 years ago and yet he is spoken about and remembered more today than then. He must have been amazing. He was. I would like to be remembered as a follower of Jesus, someone who displayed the character of Jesus' teachings.

What will you be remembered for?
Read John 3.16. 2000 years after His birth, why do so many people – 2.38 billion - follow Jesus today?

25. Clean Slate

By Stephen Read

Themes: new starts; forgiveness

The beginning of a new season is a time when all of last season's performances, both good and bad, winning and losing, are now irrelevant. Whether your team only just avoided relegation or finished top, everyone starts with a clean slate at the start of the next season.

By the end of most seasons, the team that just survived relegation will be around 50 points behind the league champions. And yet the fans of the struggling team start the new campaign on level points with the champions!

What will happen if the points weren't reset at the beginning of every season? Some teams would be hundreds of points behind by now! How would this affect their manager, players and fans?

The start of the new season is a great opportunity to sieve through the positive and negatives and start afresh. This could be committing to be punctual, encouraging others in your team and not being unhealthy during the week!

In your life do you wish that you could start again with a clean slate, forgetting all that happened before?

If we are willing to put our trust in Jesus we are offered a new beginning. Like teams at the start of the season we are offered forgiveness and help as we change the way we live.

Therefore, if anyone is in Christ, he is a new creation; old things have passed away; behold, all things have become new.

2 Corinthians 5:17

About the writers

Martin Bateman lives in Lancashire with his wife and three teenage children. He grew up in Manchester and lived through United's lows and then highs at the turn of the century. He lived overseas and worked for Operation Mobilisation for twenty years before joining Ambassadors Football in 2010. He has been British Director since 2015.

Jonathan Blair has been working as a coach for the last twenty years, trying to do he can to be good news to the world of football.

Mark Blythe is a Sports Centre Chaplain, Chelsea Foundation Walking Football Coordinator, Aussie WF International, Wembley referee and lifelong Middlesbrough fan who believes in miracles (in so many ways).

Ben Cutting is a videographer and editor for a marketing company in Birmingham having enjoyed many years as a full-time youth worker. He loves the local church and Arsenal FC.

Josh Fortune is a pastor in Woolwich, south east London. He also works for Ambassadors Football creating animated Bible stories and books.

Sam Gibb is the pastor of Hope Church Vauxhall, a church on a council estate in South London. He is a lifelong Newcastle United fan after falling in love with Kevin Keegan's Entertainers in the 90's. Sam is married to Charlie and a dad to little Judah, who will probably grow up supporting Chelsea...

Gareth Haddow worked for Ambassadors GB for 12 years before starting two years ordination training at St Mellitus Bible College in 2000. He will begin his three-year curacy training at St Paul's Shadwell in July 2022. He is married to Mich and they have three children and currently live in Stepney, Tower Hamlets. He supports Spurs.

Lucas Heubeck works as National Director for PRO11, a start-up football ministry based in Germany, part of Agape Europe.

Bronnie King is an Ambassadors staff member located in Leicester. She has played football most of her life and is passionate about seeing lives transformed by people coming to know Jesus.

Joe Lowther is married to Laura and has three sons. He is CEO of KICK, whose mission is to transform young people's lives, with God's love, through sport and support. KICK do this through values-driven physical education, street dance, mentoring, chaplaincy in schools and church-based KICK Academies to impact currently 20,000 young people per week.

Dan Owen lives in East London with his wife and two children. A former semi-pro footballer, he now oversees Ambassadors' growing number of Community Football Outreach projects.

Stephen Read is AFGB's longest serving staff member, having initially joined as an intern 15 years ago! Based at our London office, he leads a number of tournaments and playing tours, as well as local outreach projects.

Alex Shoderu is a lover of Jesus, who supports Arsenal and currently works full-time as a Secondary Chaplain in South West London.

Rob Taylor works for Ambassadors Football as National Camp Coordinator. He is a life-long Aston Villa fan and lives in Nottingham with his wife and three kids.

James Yielder is married to Lydia and father to Elijah. An avid Derby County fan, he has experienced the joys of Wembley and the despair of relegation. He works with Reign Ministries UK, helping train leaders to disciple young people across the UK.

Mark Williams is the Children and Youth worker at Copplestone Methodist Church in Mid-Devon. Married with two children, he has also been a huge Man City fan since the bad old days.

Photos by Unsplash. Thanks to

- Jeffrey F Lin
- Simon Reza
- Finn_Cdoncel
- Mitch Rosen
- Christopher Bill
- Cytonn Photography
- Nathan Rogers
- Alex
- Braden Hopkins
- Mayur Gala
- Daniel van den Berg
- Annie Spratt
- Fikri Rasvid
- Stephen Hately
- Edge2Edge Media
- Abigail Keenan
- Dan Parker
- Sandro Schuh
- Ali Yaqub
- Charisse Kenion
- Kelly Repreza
- Fauzan Saari
- Connor Coyne
- Ffion Grosse

About Ambassadors Football

Ambassadors Football's vision is to serve the local church, inspiring and equipping it to build Christ-centred relationships through football. We want to invest in churches and invest in people to share Jesus through football. We are involved in leading:

- Community Football Outreach projects and training
- Football camps
- Internships
- Coaching and playing tours
- Resources
- Outreach tournaments

To hear more and explore how you or your church might be involved, visit https://gb.ambassadorsfootball.org or contact gb@ambassdorsfootball.org

AMBASSADORS
FOOTBALL

Printed in Great Britain
by Amazon

80854710R00058